SCENES IN BETWEEN A CURSE AND A DREAM

A POETRY COLLECTION

Dedicated to the bestest momma in the whole wide world and the bestest little sister ever! My air beneath my wings and my discipline within.

Table of contents

I Know

I know in which direction I am to head in life,
based on the poem my soul is able to write.

When the sun extends its rays, or
when the stars shine bright.

Those long peaceful days, or
those short restless nights.

A path to servitude, or
a path to conquer which will enable strife.

I know in which direction I am to head in life,
based on the poem my soul is able to write.

Kronos

When I am in America,
I do not walk around my neighborhood unless,
I have my German Sheppard/Lab mix puppy with me.

Mada! Me nuh kno weh deh bally da foreign deh pan!
So four paws and a wagging tail becomes an unconcealed weapon to see.

I consider myself a cool, peaceful soul,
but my oppressor's shells are not empty.

So, I respectfully give them their own space, intentionally seeking to remain
displaced. For my neighbors land is a land where roaming souls are mostly
empty.

They tempt me as I leave my home.
A mouse trap for a stranger in a foreign zone.

A sacrificial lamb to their cause,
and all that is needed, is for me to walk alone.

But I remain in stride,
ears open with my head held high.

My puppy keeps looking back to check on me, while leading the pace with
pride.

We turn corners like we are drifting.
Our motion interrupted only by his pissing and his sniffing.

My neighbors do remain disappointed,
due to his presence not being missing.

I remain aware of what exists around me.
My success impedes these enemies' boundaries.

So as I stroll to release the weight of society's toll.
May a pup with a God's name be the entity that protects me.

It is written

It is written that, sometimes, the punishment must occur before the crime.
Currently living in an answered prayer, I say.

Of the days long departed, to the ones that are to come.
Please, just bring peace my way.

To every instance of being an instant blessing.
To balance the curses per mistakes I have made.

To every demon whose demonstrations earned their slaughter,
Cheers to the beings of divinity who have illuminated my way.

But enough of the disharmonious discourse.
For you are here to be moved.

But let us keep our audible tones low.
For we know who lurks under this moon.

All that I ask is that you pay attention, for this life's imminent presentation,
will be nothing less than a transformation.

So as man turns to beast, these scenes that you will witness seeks no end.

Now get ready dear friends, at any moment this enigmatic energy of a being
can signal, it is ready to begin.

Hear ye, Hear ye

Hear ye, hear ye!
To thou I scream!
Lend me an audible ear,
bear witness to what I have seen."

> "Hear ye, hear thee!
> To thou I scream!
> Lend me an audible ear,
> bear witness to what I have seen."

"Hear ye, hear me!
To thou I scream!
Lend me an audible ear,
bear witness to what I have seen."

The path of an emerald enchantress,
just intersected with that of a beast who feared no foe.

Her powers of elemental enchantments and visions and spells.
His, a mere passive ability to weaken those who oppose, those who impede,
those who delay, the route to where he must go.

With such a great ability,
there is no need for him to strike.

For any attempts to physically impair him,
only takes away from one own's might.

But...

On the other side of sight, the emerald enchantress appeared to take flight.
She summoned wings so white they glowed in the night.

Her mystic crystals formed a shield,
while sage incubated her from evils that strayed from the light.

Within her lies an eagerness that is unresolved, as if harmony of this world is her day job.
As she glides in stride, she felt an energy from afar.

And I quote what she spoke,

"Never before! Can it be? Someone as nearly as powerful as me?
I must know who they are!

Meanwhile…

Wounded from battle, the beast lay in his cave.
See, success has a price that must be paid.

As he heals it is revealed that such cycles will be consistent with the rest of his days.

Such a gift is this burden, to manifest as he is learning.
To gain prestige as he is serving, only to return it and spurn them.
For all treasures of this world are not worth earning.

Aware of an intruder, he shuddered a warning.

"The beast has a sense of hearing that is very acute, so although I cannot see,
 I can hear you.

How dare you of a fool to enter my domain and disturb my zen that is peaceful".

The enchantress then speaks…

"I mean you no harm pleasant beast,
but your mission attracted me.

I've had great visions, I have seen,
all of your scenes in between a curse and a dream.

You are the one they speak of, the one with no name.
Our origins are different, but our mission is the same.
Protect the ones we love, serve all who remain.

But there is one final mission called love,
and for that mission dear beast, you are afraid of."

"Hello!! Hello!!", I snap back to reality, as a blank stare covers my face.

"Oh, I am so sorry, I did not hear anything, you were trying to say.
I got lost in your eyes and started to dream during the day."

Fear Vs Love

Peacefully, I've been swimming in the shallows.
The repercussions of a fear for being emotionally deep.

The safety of knowing that emotionally, my feet are touching the ground.
The setting of a moonlit night, with waves crashing against the beach.

Over the sea's horizon I see, a silhouette walking towards thee.
With my vision being less than acute, all that is being witnessed in the
distance, is this shadowy figure in front of me.

In elapsed time we collide, me and this figure eye to eye.
I am petrified of the events of this night but the real scare,
is seeing that this figure is,
                              is,
                                  is,
                                      I.

A man that I've bottled up on the inside, has escaped his imprisonment.
His hope for love, has kept him alive.

Now, this battle must ensue.

A man who fears yielding to love, versus one that is very lovable.
One who has a heartful of emotions, versus one who is very hard to talk to.

One who prefers to keep conversations in the shallows, versus one who isn't
afraid of the conversations that are deep.
Nemesis during a stare down, they both understand the heart will bleed,
nevertheless, the battle proceeds.

The man with fear strikes first!
He's reminded of past pains, he's afraid of future hurts.
A blow so direct, it sends the man of love to the dirt.
Fear grimaces with a smirk, for surely a strike so powerful,
would bury any hope of love in a hearse.

Meanwhile…

Fighting what seemed to be his twin.
Maybe it is his doppelganger, raised by a necromancer,
the man of love was unsure of his enemy's origins.
All that he knew was that he was tired of being locked in.
For control of this mind, body and soul, this battle, he must win.

As his face rest in the sand, he started to realize that he can.
Give his heart, escape the shallows and become more than a man.
On my feet I stand, I will not be defeated by fear, let it be proclaimed
throughout the land.

The man of love is now upright, the cowardly reflection of himself within his
sight. "This battle is not over", he states, "only one of us shall survive this
night."

Towards each other they run full speed.
Fear versus love, the shallows versus the deep, for control of me, who shall it
be?

An epic collision of emotions causes a cataclysm on this beach.

But who is the victor? We shall see.

For the last scene before the dream was over,
was that of the man of love asking the man of fear to yield.

"Damn you fear!"
"Let me be!"
"I must show, how much love is within me!"
"I must show, I do not fear getting deep!"
"So why won't you yield!?"
"Fear! Why won't you yield!?"
WHY
WON'T
YOU
YIELD!?

Grow

Eat the knowledge and grow.

We already told you what to do, so why are you bothering us for?
Reaps of insight are to be expected, when depths of servitude are sewed.

Now, eat the knowledge and grow.

For the soul should never take score.
Immortals entangled with mortals, so on an even higher vibration we must go.

Caves and abyss, peaks filled with mist, as a waterfall dives it is realized,
we are of a few walking, the last of a species not known to exist.

What madness of a riddle is this?

An answer we may not know points the direction to where we must go.
Although it is written that the path to enlightenment one must never show.

Just, eat the knowledge and grow.

Dear Mr. Poet

One day after a show, I got approached by audience members,
who perceived me to be slow. As if, even with directions in my hands, I would
not know where to go.

They proceeded to ask me the following questions.

"Dear Mr. Poet,
How does the intentional use of language development and scribing practices
provide us access to rigorous poetry content?"

I replied, while stuck in a scene in between a curse and a dream.

"As a result of our conversation, it is clear that writing is necessary
to increase the rigor and elevate our cognitive aptitude within.

It builds an elevated corridor for capacity in which one can access, maintain
and achieve levels of accomplishments that will strategically navigate the host
to success.

Fulfillment creates nourishment by self.

Elaborations of descriptions, models the way we walk, the way we talk.

Use any background knowledge one has attained.
These tools will assist in speaking and writing as exploration will only lead to
discussions.
Doing so makes you an expert on any language function, so brainstorm
different applications of your purpose.

But truth be told,

I have been speaking nonsense from the start, just let your emotions carry your
heart and simply write down your thoughts."

I was then asked,

"Dear Mr. Poet, how does nonfiction work?"
I replied, "they are merely scenes in between a curse and a dream.

A stranger said she prayed for me and in doing so, her heart burned.
I looked up while walking my pup, I could see ufo's turn.
Shooting stars, double rainbows, for what next, my soul yearns.

"Unlike my last journey", those words are written on my left arm.
I remember the state of mind, the burden, the push, that I have to move on.
One could never imagine the storms, the land, the path that I originated from.

I awake in the morning bruised and battered from battle.
Astral travel by my subconscious while I am unconscious.
Knots in my back, crooks in my neck, scars, the absence of breath awakes me.

I must be within its grasp, but my story was spoken by the future,
that a long life I will have.

So, you want to know how nonfiction works?

Well, its roots are instituted with truth. I elaborate not to exaggerate,
but to paint a clear perception to you.

Let the audible phonics you hear, be your guide, be your steer
and without any presence of fear,

Walk with me,
Walk with me,
Walk with me."

Murderers

Shhhh
They are murderers, without even knowing they are,
murderers, without even knowing they are.

Why do some people make existence so painful?
Why do they make it hard to survive in life?
Just to win we must roll the dice, then get the same number twice.

It is, as if, we are, mice trapped in a maze, wasting our days, saying prayers,
running away from our fears, knowing that it will only catch up to us over the
years.

We only have one life to live, but that life I would give up so fast.
Just to get a gasp of another life that I know I could never have.

To be free of pain? There is no one person I can blame,
for giving it to me so, I just have to, let it be, patiently, wait and see
if they continue giving this pain to me.

I know they will but still,
lack the courage to tell them, that emotionally, I have been killed.

Murderers, without even knowing they are, *shhhh,* they are
murderers, without even knowing they are.

The Beetle

It is amazing and scary, to see all the punishment,
a human body can take, before it concedes to lady death.

Once, I found a beetle.
I proceeded to place this beetle on a piece of paper.
I then dropped the paper in a bucket of water.

I sat there watching the beetle try to escape,
knowing I had her destiny on my finger.

I watched it go under the paper, looking for a way out,
then coming back on top to catch some air.

She did this numerous times before she gave up.

I watched her floating around in the water,
knowing her final moments were a few seconds away.

I threw another piece of paper in the water, so the beetle could crawl on.
She did and once again, she tried to find a way out, thinking that there *was* a
way out.

I went away, forgetting about the beetle.
When I came back, I saw her floating in the water.
I knew she was dead and I knew I had killed it.

I sometimes wonder about all the punishment my body has taken in this thing called life.

Then I say to myself, "how and why am I still alive?"

I sometimes wonder if someone is doing the same thing to my life, that I did to that beetle.

With me always trying to find a way out, knowing the only way out, is?

My brother, My brother

*2 Glock forty fives, identical twins, when they sing it is a beautiful harmony,
identical hymns. But the sin is knowing that...*

My brother, my brother, the Devil has some ammo too.
My brother, my brother, do not let that ammo be you.

Is it better to be the Devil's right-hand man, than to be standing in his way?
Can you believe these words were written on the Lord's day?

As I started to write, a black widow crossed my path.
Maybe I was being warned about writing words, I should not have.

The ink in the pen, although full, did not want to put itself on the paper.
I thought it knew the repercussions of what may happen later.

My brother, my brother, there is a war going on.
The Devil is prepared and all the while we think he is living in fear.
See the Devil has some that will worship him, others that will die for him.

May I ask, will you die for your Lord? I hope that question does not seem
absurd.

See the Devil has some, that will kill themselves, to kill you.
Yes, the Devil has some ammo too. My brother, my brother,
do not let that ammo be you.

You see my brother, with truth being told.

There is no right or wrong, only perception.
As human beings, we can only hope not to act on pure emotions.

So, what is reasoning? When we have negativity in our hearts.
And the death of another brother, is the only occupant residing in our
thoughts.

Aristotle believed our words are more powerful than our weapons.
So why do we choose weapons when the negative starts to happen?

My brother, my brother, I am not God, so I cannot say killing is morally
wrong.
But it can only be right, when hell freezes over,
and we are ice skating on the Amazon.

My brother, my brother, the Devil has some ammo too.
But my brother, my brother, please, do not let that ammo be you.

Round Three

The speech comes in a low tone to maintain your focus.
But the baritones with or without a microphone, just put that clitoris on notice.

I don't know if you know this, but when that pressure gets released,
splash waterfalls on these sheets, we shall see what we conceive.

For this is not a sex poem, just a process of creation that must be believed.
A miracle of a baby girl or baby boy, I just want to enjoy planting that seed.

Love, I know you are weak, but you must stop shaking at the knees.
It is time for round three.

Round one? Round one was all about me, about how I have grown from the life of selfishness and foolery.

About why it was necessary for only me to eat, when there is a feast to feed,
but because of greed, I caused starvation for the family.

Never again shall I maintain a state of being emotionless.

Calls for distress, the distant S.O.S, I looked away from the wrecks,
for it simply was not worth my stress.

I didn't even shed tears when they laid loved ones to rest.

But round two? Round two is all about you, yeah, I said you beautiful.
About how you managed to make an empty creature full.

About how you took no bullshit, a solid queen as you stood still,
you did not even flinch when being charged by this bull.

It is crazy yet sexy how you kept your cool.

Your warmth faded my cold, I was built rough around the edges so I would never fold.

Days of the future can wait as I grow old, for all I want in the world is,
my soul,
    your soul,
        melting souls,
            make us whole,
                on one knee,
                    I propose,
                        babe say yes,
                            say I am yours.

Round three? Round three is all about we, about what this union can be, about a love that can outlast an eternity.

Generational wealth is across the street, for us to keep, but in unison we must move our feet.

Blessed is our home, but we must be a blessing to those in need.

Our child can create lifelong smiles, make that two if you are down for the ride. As long as they have your attitude, your passions, your desires. I will be the protector so fear no wild.

For round three is where I plan to proceed, in creating us, a child.

Truth be told

It takes more than a nice ass, a pretty face, round tits to impress me.

Trust, the finest lips has been wrapped around this dick.
To fill my appetite, I have sampled different delicacies of my cross-globe trips.

Back when I was wondering about where the cash was at, it was all about where the next piece of ass is at, mentally mature, now I am pass that.

You see, the old me, slowly, is only available via flashback.
So I will pause on that life and let these youngsters have that.

If you were to ask me, "what are you cooking tonight?" Truth be told, my response would be to let you know the entrées listed on my cooking menu are minimal.

We are ordering takeout tonight.

I am only five foot eleven but being ten toes down makes me stand taller on sight.

You will get to respect my might, but babe, a bird with one wing cannot take flight. So, if it is real, then let me feel, because these scenes, seems right.

Truth be told, even a healed man has scars.

The ones on the surface, those are from the journeys near.
But those deep ones, those are from the journeys afar.

Place your hands on my heart.
Feel this rhythm I want us to dance to forever, all you have to do is play your part and it is looking like right now, is a damn good time to start.

Truth be told, these days, I cannot put myself first.
You see my mind is not always right.

At this age, I figured, I would have already made the ride in that black hearse.
But thanks to you, these days are filled with light.

Obstructions were planted to see me reverse,
but for that protection, I pray at night.

Now as the world gives me the recognition they think I deserve.

I give the most high credit, I will just take an extension of life on this earth,
with a woman that is worthy of carrying my child, until childbirth.

Do not call me your superman, that title means nothing to me.
How about you call me your man and watch your life change drastically.

Girl, if the feeling is the same, then let me change your last name.

Together, we will build a kingdom that shall remain.
We have what it takes to eliminate dead weight, but our path must be the
same.

Truth be told, when all is revealed, you shall see.

You do not need tarots to tell you the future,
for what is to come will ask you what you want it to be.

And all I want you to tell the days of the future,
is that you want it to be with me.

Saturday

A queen sits to my right, her physique rests sleek, body frame sits tight.
Her mystique gives me might, so it is only right that I ask.
Hey love, is Saturday cool? Let us say evening also? Dinner, drinks and a vibe.

As I turn off the ambient noise near my heart,
I hear the unstoppable and the unmovable collide.

I have never been one to believe things are supposed to last,
so hidden beneath many layers, this heart resides.

But girl your eyes, your smile, those lips, your style,
yields a yearn, a desire, motivation, light my fire.

When you whisper words to my ear, that kitten purrs to her bear.
What world? Disappear! You are my girl, let them hear it.

Saturday's cool? Let us say evening also?
dinner, drinks and a vibe.

Oh, so it is cool? Well let me know if there is anything you do not eat.
They say pleasure comes with pain, so, for the rough times, I apologize
beforehand, I have warned thee.

Your facial expression is looking like you are ready to put me in position.
I am talking about rings and things, whips and trips, in your country, my
country, no limitations to our world, all you have to do is, be my girl.

So, is Saturday cool? Let us say evening also? Dinner, drinks and a vibe

She then speaks...

" I will consider making you my boo.
The man I might want to drink a few with while taking in views, vibing entails
good moods, skip the line, first in que.

Boy I will hold you down, massage your heart, merge our souls,
things simplified, cruise control.

So, do not keep me waiting in line.
On Saturday, I just want to have a good time, unwind, sip on some wine and
see if that heart of yours, melt in these eyes of mine".

I can quote my mother

I can quote my mother saying that when I was young,
I did not enjoy walking on the sidewalk, I preferred walking in the road.
I was never disobedient, I was just very bold.
I was an adolescent, whose mind was very old.
I was warm at the heart but at the flesh,
I was very, very, cold.

During sunsets I reminisce about what I used to be.
My resiliency allowed for slight irresponsibility's.

Genuinely, I can say, I am wrong in life for destroying things that had
meaning to me.

You see,

this mental state of seeing nothing but warfare on my plate,
had me eating hate! Unable to reconciliate, so I regurgitate,
a false image of my,
        of my,
            of myself,
and when I murdered them was the only time they came to congratulate!
Oh, what cold hands did they shake.

But on this day, I can honestly say, it was a good day.
We are still in stride on this side.

Yesterday I met a good guy who hit my car causing an accident
while driving down the street at five, I am glad we both survived.

Earlier I avoided spies from the other side who dare not look me in the eye.
See, the undignified are denied vacancy to reside in the dwelling of the five.

That is the five percent nation, if you know, you know.

They believe, only five percent of the world sees the truth. Eighty five percent
are mere puppet on strings, simply doing what they are told. The remaining
ten percent, are their puppet masters, controlling the eighty-five percents
mind, body and soul. Oh, what evil creations do they mold.

But you must believe that my God has an army too.
And on the front lines, stands this new recruit.

Accepting of a suicide mission, yes, I would die for you.
If that is what it takes, for you to see the truth.

I can now quote my mother saying how proud she is of who she sees.
Thank you, peace, for letting things be.

No longer in denial, this guy now rises with a smile, for outlasting the trails,
of this journey's last mile.

A Deep Thought

An item only exists, by what it is perceived.
And within its midst, lies what we believe.

Outliers lay insignificant, away from relativity.
And feelings of confidence makes way to insecurity.

Its true definition, one shall never find.
For this is the last hour, so little time.

Its thoughts, its meaning, dwindling down the line.
And the search so difficult, like a deep·thought, in a shallow mind.

The Lone Wolf

*You see, I had to become a lone wolf, for wolves' hunt in packs and I hunt no
more.*
The sheep must be fed.
*That is a role where I can succeed, serving a divine purpose, trusting none
other than me.*

"Hey Mr. I like your dog," he said with a smile so innocent and divine.
"Thank you" I said, quickly to reply,
"Is he a K9?" He asked as his face radiated with glee.
"Well, he is half Lab, half German Sheppard, so that makes him half K9
right?" His head shook up and down so fast, I could envision his future
success being commemorated on a bubblehead night.

*The path of the lone wolf steers steady, a linear sequential order of essential
steps, be his guide.*

"Excuse me, is this machine open?" Health is wealth they say,
so I have decided to hit the gym, on this beautiful lord given day.
I must make sure the glow on the outside, matches the peace that resides
within.
"Mr., Mr.!", I know that cadence, a reverberation that is all too familiar.
Looking up I see him, a student who just recently exited my class,
graduating to the next level in life, seeking what he has never had.
"Are you ready for high school?" My words are interrupted, for he prefers the
love of a hug. His parents can only smile as we get back to how we were.

*The shoulder of the lone wolf grows strong, absent are the draining,
insufficient nourishment, the weight of the pack can put on.*

"So, we have been hearing you are the guy to come speak to about building
strong relationships with the students."
I reply, "In other words, you heard that I am good at controlling the worst of
our classes?"
I look them both dead in the eye, two men that were strong with brawn,
but for what is to come, their timidness took the stage.
"I tell you what", I said, "You want the student's cosign?
Meet me across the street, one hundred dollars' worth of breakfast burritos,
we will make sure they all eat.

Bring some sneakers to play ball or you can stand off to the side but make
sure your presence is big and tall.
Be vulnerable to any stumble, teach them resilience if they may fall."

*The lone wolf howls towards the full moon of the night.
Good deeds were done, great examples were set, the daily peace earned has
filled his appetite.*

Belize City, Belize

Just from the look in his eye,
his killers could tell that he knew something.

The way his legs were bound, the way his hands were tied when they ignited
that fire, the scene ended gruesome.

Around here, because of fear, we are raised to keep knots tight around necks.
No need to loose them, with these words I might lose some.

But the slums I am from constructed a petrified mind, illuminating perilous
scenes, so, I will try not to confuse them.

Now, that previous scene might seem hard to some.
But you see, where I am from, your local news broadcast will never come.

Guns are rung making the sound of drums.
Everyday a mother mourns a son.

In a land where those other than demons fear to come, there is no need to run.

So, we just grab a gun, drink until numb, as we let ganja smoke fill our lungs.

Now please don't be stupid, thinking these rude boys will not do it,
to see someone leaking red fluid.

On Instagram live, some will still do it, pull it.
Some C-walk, some Piru it, Gangster Disciples, Vice Lords, vatos locos,
if you know the G code, then you are cool with.

Not much effort, less attitude,
by design I am a creature of solitude.

17 degrees north, 88 degrees west, Belize City, Belize.
These coordinates showed me how to find resolution.

But such a shame on what I have become,
this world is a mere jungle, these beasts are caged in.

And mi bwoi
Da sin da sin
Tin chance fuh win
Di game wi di play in
Ah link mi bredren
Tell him to stay in
Mi balli, wicked tingz a gwaan
Even Babylon is sprayin

That is a visual from the other side,
we are from different worlds,
but out here the same truth collides.

Fools with their guns will have their fun,
while looking in the white of our eyes.

R.I.P. to all the victims of gun homicide.

Certain experiences can close the differences between you and I.

May our experiences close the distance between you and I.

Untitled

A wandering soul is permissible to exist in many worlds.

I must now depart yours although leaving in gratitude,
shall be written as these last words.

So special are the days when energies of attraction connects.
Meanwhile a comet leads way to where astrological maps are being set.

The people we have met embrace the displace from our natural home.
Earth's topography merely reveals that heaven is a ceiling to a universe's dome.

It saddens thee that these unfortunate roads allowed me to learn what is
claimed to be unknown, even E.T. was allowed to phone home, why was I
told to just carry on?

Weary and thin but still committed to the journey within.

To travel to worlds where it is expected for the wind to sing.
Please let this cold rain kiss my skin.

To generalize what I now realize to be a life full of lies is not fair to you and I.

So let my words form an apology, with the sincerity,
that resides from a place beyond horizons eyes.

In peace I depart your world.

A stranger turned friend but bloodlines were never sewed.
For people of the sun shall never exist with the people of the snow.

On this journey we both must go.
Now, eat the knowledge and grow.

This Is Just a Test

Mic check one two one two, this is just a test, this is just a test.

The African slave trade started over money!
This is just a test; this is just a test.
Conquerors selling their conquered to oppressors for milk and honey!
This is just a test; this is just a test.

Black folks watching black folks go hungry,
trust there isn't shit about that funny.

For if they came together, create spawns,
forever there would be no end to this money.

But this is just a test; this is just a test.

Black wall street defined all odds, black folks to the world,
were once again seen as gods.

But due to the cards being dealt, odds being felt,
these days it is all a façade.

They would rather go to war against each other,
than to recognize what they truly are.

Testing, testing

Some still exist from when they marched.
The precedent was set by others long departed but remain in our hearts.

The black dollar shall forever exist in unity,
but because they are divided, they starve. But,

this is just a test; this is just a test

Real love sees no race, creed or gender!
Yes, this is just a test; this is just a test.
But your gods, your culture, makes y'all prisoners, so please surrender!
Y'all emotional vultures!
Trying to take what is not yours!
This peace that I've worked for!
These days that I want more!
To preserve I would want war!
I nuh ramp wid pikni,
suh I deh dah yuh front door!

Mic check one two one two,
this is just a test; this is just a test.

Being from a distant land,
I never knew you needed a marriage license to get married.

This is just a test; this is just a test.

My first union was all fraud!
Muscled up for my green card!
Battle the feds and remain scarred!
I low key just snitched on myself real hard.
I am not a poet, I do not read bars,
I just vent to y'all real hard,
Through transparency I recharge,
I just hope that this energy reach y'all.
Because mic check one two, you know the rest.

This is just a test; this is just a test.

Breaths

{DEEP SLOW INHALE}
{DEEP SLOW EXHALE} … Breath I

As I decent into unconsciousness, frightful images of life appear.
Failure, immaturity, desperation and in witnessing such, I scare.

The thin line has been broken, damage far beyond repair.
This life's bitterfull agony, I shall endure for years.

So, spare the sincerity, do not approach with glee.
Let letters form words of truth, speak negative upon me.

A façade is my reality, for it appeared never as it seemed.
For never was I truly, the once and future king.

{DEEP SLOW INHALE}
{DEEP SLOW EXHALE}…Breath 2

Of what once was, shall occur today.
For I have learned as much from the wrongs, as the rights of my ways.

With resiliency I have endured, humility within preserved.
My birthright is a blessing, courtesy of our lord.

{DEEP SLOW INHALE}
{DEEP SLOW EXHALE} ... Breath 3

The rebirth of flesh, in the season of shedding.
With one final breath, the right direction I am heading.

Being once a boy, I have put away childish things.
For in the man I have become, I need not such things.

For the new path being paved, consistency shall guide.
Unlike my last journey, where I walked with closed eyes.

For when you live and you learn, wisdom does follow.
And on this journey, I see the better tomorrow.

For just over the horizon, lies a great land.
And within its occupancy, lies a great man.

{DEEP SLOW INHALE} ...

My Two Best Friends

When I am lonely,
when I have no one to hold me.

I call on my two best friends,
paper and pen.

They keep me happy, satisfied and occupied,
for with them, there is nothing for me to hide.

When there is no way to express my feelings,
they always seem to perceive what I am seeing.

Even without a mouth to talk or ears to hear,
when I need them, they are always there.

Maybe if they had a choice, they would not be here.
But sometimes it seems like they are, the only ones who care.

When I have a lot on my mind, but do not know what to say.
I call on my two best friends.

For they are the only ones who I know will be there for me,
again and again.

The External Rain, Hail, Sleet, Snow

Being in a state of judgement before knowledge,
an inopportune destination awaits.

The cold of a winter's nightfall remains,
as I feel the warmth of my new fate.

Internal fire turns blood to lava,
insignificance is extinguished by that molten flow.

For that fire within shall never dull,
no matter the external rain, hail, sleet, snow.

Do not look back fellow stranger,
expectations can be found far or near.

Satisfaction through nonverbal communication,
may take days, weeks, months, or even years.

What is that you hear? 'Tis a howling sound,
a siren claims to be an alarm.

Lack of concern to where it is from,
trepidation towards where it is going.

Dihydrogen Monoxide

In all this madness,
I first off want to thank you all for attending this debriefing this evening.

So as far as the anomaly we were able to witness earlier.
All that is known at this moment is that the source of the entity,
is a projection within a written journal.

We will proceed to document and record the events,
 as being transcribed on this day.

Now let it be understood that obtaining these words did not come easy.

For only during the Samhain, it is predicted, that what we will hear is
scheduled to appear.

We will begin with informing you that,
it was branded with what now seems to be the letter "M".
Located near what we would consider to be dear, a heart.

A sigil of a spell must have been casted,
For its voice, from its body, it doesn't, it wouldn't, it couldn't, depart.

At the time of documentation it was feasting on meat,
although it was not currently in a state of hunger.

We now recognize the letter "M" that was previously stamped,
was a permission of passage to the land of us,
what it considered to be the land of mortals.

During an encounter to a familiar place, it sensed stimulations,
leading it to witness the events described thus far.

First off were celestial goddesses using elements to create life from glass.
We will proceed by naming that creation art.

It observed a form of spell work, sorcery, witchcraft, from an imposter angel,
making potions from the other side of what seems to be an alcoholic bar.

On a night for witches, it knew the line was thin,
So, it focused on the mission to reveal the limitations that keeps us apart.

It chose the path of most resistance, as of yet, we are not sure why it chose
this route.
But we are assuming a lack of our dimensional intelligence

Although it must be noted, it had the awareness to know that its survival,
was dependent on dihydrogen monoxide.
What we here on this plane of existence would consider to be, water.

A Mortal's Tale

The sun sets in the west, but it must rise in the east.
And during the winter's nightfall you can witness a beast of Belize.

Tales from deep, echoed by tongues from afar.
The stories to be told this night, shall be emboldened to all.

How dare ye label me a mere man! Human men?
Thee is nothing like them! I am less than a celestial but much more than a king!

I have dwelled with fairies, elves, vampires, witches' spells!
I have witnessed beings of darkness hell itself has expelled!

But on ye journey a unique entity was seen from while to while.
For even the creatures of the deep were timid amongst this beast of the wild.

With a grip, a tilt of reality, power to turn the world on its side.
Evidence only to be discovered when one decides to realize.

Belief can vanish, known truths can be dressed in disguise.
As for this peaceful soul, the return his armor for one last ride.

The Gift

Existence that has finally shone, true colors that are finally known.
The race is not for the swift, vision is the gift, to the lion that is finally grown.

Obstacles can be seen from the blind side, only time can make you wise.
Program your eyes to be perceptive, true worth's value lies in the skies.

It has begun, the war proceeds, to the victor awaits Valhalla.
Pace can't be undone, leave the meager and weak, peace has entered the battle.

Every Twelfth Day

I know why thorns have roses; I know why the caged bird sings.
I know why you had to leave but I know I need to see you again.

I know I will miss you while you are gone, but this pain is a little different.
A hurt of a son without a mom, and the thought of not having you with me.

You once gave me hell, now that thought is hard to believe.
You had me feeling powerless, wondering how long it takes the heart to heal.

Now, I am barely making it without you, without seeing your face,
and I cry when I hear your voice, on every twelfth day.

But sacrifices must be made, you are absolutely making a strong one.
I do not know how you are doing, but your son is struggling.

In short, I miss you, surely, that is needless to say.
Because it is the eleventh and I will tell you so, on the twelfth day.

Heaven

The grass is greener on this side, for the opposite are the roots.
Oh, what an unpleasant view for my eyes, if it was not for you.

My destiny is fulfilled, for you said it to me.
With honesty and passion, but most importantly sincerity.

Faith is never seen, except for what I view.
For faith is in the physical form, of the one that says, "I love you too."

Words from the heart, in essence, are in their purest form.
And the eyes of the one who reads this, was of heaven born.

I thank you, for being a difference maker in my world.
And for proving that God, allows his angels to exist,
in the form of a girl.

Sunday Morning Sunrise

circle one, choose one, choose wisely

Sunday Morning sunrise, what a beautiful day to be alive.
What is the purpose of buying a rose, eventually knowing that it will die?

We all have hope / faith for the best, expecting hope / faith to be on our side.
That is when our faith and our hope, as combatants, collide.

While they both lead, they each have their contingent of followers.
Consistent advertising, now which belief is more genuine to their customers?

In my many years of existence, there is one thing that I have learned.
That having hope or believing in faith, is no longer a big concern.

Anything done in this world, is done by hope / faith, it may not seem that way.
But when the sun goes down, I have hope / faith, that it will rise the next day.

A Touch of Nature

A Woodpecker and a Blue Jay coexist in the tree above me

Bees are pollinating flower to flower at my feet

I think a squirrel just threw a nut at me

A touch of nature how these days give me peace

A Little Control

A little control in a world full of chaos.
On the inside I am lonely, on the outside I play it off.

Silence is a virtue, so, I act on it.
And in the presence of opportunity, I pass on it.

She then walks by, turns around, smiles at me.
Whispering quietly, this is the reason why you are lonely.

This Clear Liquid

Where would mankind be without electricity?
Or those with fins in the sea without their water to breathe?

Humanitarians have their love for one another.
The faithful hold their belief in a higher power.

Even the powerful do not have full control over their health
All the while the rich are baptizing in their humanly wealth

As for me, when I take that trip towards the blue sky.
I will have this clear liquid in my eyes.

Still hearing the whispers of those saying.
Now that he is dead, I am glad that he died.

On The Pitch

This is an example of the excellence we are accustomed to expecting. The result is high excitement, until one gets fouled. It will be difficult to win the tactical matchup and we know some will stay at home. Take the time to break down the high pressure, besides, it is the ire that is significant in the scene. As it is nested somewhere in between a curse and a dream.

The combatant apologizes as he makes contact, he realizes that to grow is not a free trip. A lot of questions must be answered, ye shall be the payee of these tickets.

It is turning out to be a pleasant evening, with the rain long gone. A benevolent feeling marks a great spot, no lack of outlets to restrict thee on. But life offers a late challenge, worthy of a few words. I see why you do not want the pacing; the momentum is leaving you behind. What do I see before me? Opportunities are at a premium. When you have set the standard for so long, they expect you to follow them.

SCENES IN BETWEEN A CURSE AND A DREAM

END

About the author

Jamaal Rocke or Mr. Rocke as he is called by his students, Is a captivating author, dedicated teacher and community advocate. Originally from Belize City, Belize, he embarked on an inspiring journey to the United States during adolescence, bringing with him a passion for writing and performing poetry. He combines his love for education with his commitment to serving the youth, making a profound impact within and beyond the classroom. Engaged in his community, Mr. Rocke actively uplifts others through various initiatives, embodying the true spirit of a mentor. He is currently rooted in St. Petersburg, Florida,